Your Project Needs You

John Chapman

Your Project Needs You

Published by Completelynovel.com

First published in the UK in 2017 by CompletelyNovel

https://completelynovel.com/

ISBN 978-1-7872-3189-4

Printed in the UK by Lightning Source

Cover Design by brenda_art177
https://www.fiverr.com/brenda_art177

Follow John on Twitter: @chapmanjs

A series of educational videos, blogs and other items of interests are available at:
https://www.youtube.com/user/theprogrammedirector

Praise for Your Project Needs You

I was delighted to review John's latest assortment of blogs covering a broad spectrum of topics from classical writers to football and so much more. John has an intelligent, poignant and crisp writing style. All his blogs have been carefully selected by a project management practitioner at the top of his game. John's research is meticulous and his use of metaphors and analogies help paint a richly descriptive picture that demand time for thoughtful personal reflection.

The infamous American author and humourist Mark Twain once said in an apologetic note to a colleague, "I didn't have time to write a short letter, so I wrote a long one instead". The beauty of John's blogs are that they have been shortened to create maximum impact and that's exactly what they do. They stimulate a reaction of the type that is healthy for the mind, soul and spirit. I commend them to you.

Dr James Dale DCrimJ, MBA, RPP FAPM, FCIPD, DMS, CIM.

As always, it was a pleasure to read John's work and a delight to see the range of blogs combined into a collection and ordered compendium. A great reference for quick 'project pick me ups'.

John's writing style is ideal for those short on time, or for those who need an anecdote to help digest a concept. For example, Chapter 15 "The Scapegoat" is one that stopped and made me think - how often are our projects really open and collaborative? Do project teams work in fear of being a scapegoat if something goes wrong, or are they empowered to speak up early. The Scapegoat job description made me chuckle, and helped reinforce the points John raised - informative and funny, excellent!

I recommend this book to all working in the project management community, and wider. There are a lot of suggestions and thought provoking arguments that will stop and make you think - 'why don't I do that; that would work for me; great idea!'. Here is a challenge for readers of this book - read and digest, and then choose one topic to apply to your project... and see what you can change. Then let us all know by writing a blog post.

Dr Edward Wallington

Former Chair of APM Programme Management SIG

This is a delightful gem of a book. Each chapter takes a couple of minutes at most to read and its style reminds me of Zen Buddhism's koans and stories: you read, reflect and think how the lesson could apply to you.

And if you do that, then each anecdote or comparison can only make you a better project manager – or a better person for that matter – and this is what you will become. As such, I recommend you don't rush this book, but savior it. Say a chapter a day to read, reflect and apply

Alternatively, use it as if John is your personal Zen Buddhist monk! Consult with it when you want a different perspective that will make you think.

Either way, enjoy it and develop yourself.

Dr Jon Broome, Managing Consultant,
Leading Edge Project Consulting Ltd
Previous chair of the Association for Project Management's Contracts and Procurement SIG.

Your projects need you and you need to read this book.

This set of articles of John's are a must read for project managers. Combining several different topics and a simple and creative set of examples, he portraits the many aspects of the life of a project manager, including the ultra-relevant aspects of leadership, communications and culture in the project environment.

The articles allow the reader to reflect and understand the different dimensions of one of the most complex tasks of today's environment: get things done. I am sure you will enjoy the reading like I enjoyed!

Ricardo Viana Vargas
2009 Chairman, PMI Board of Directors
Writer and blogger on Project Management & Strategy
Executive Director of Brightline Initiative

As I read John Chapman's book, Roger von Oech's creative thinking strategy came to mind: *A Whack on the Side of the Head.* We can get so blinkered in our habitual thinking that we need writers like John to bring us all an abrupt sideways perspective. He challenges some tired old assumptions and looks afresh at what we are doing.

For example, we get sloppy in using the word 'meeting' too much - and, perhaps, in meeting too much. John suggests we can shake this up somewhat with some imaginative words that could lead to better outcomes.

The reader will find simple but powerful metaphors throughout as well as lyrical similes such as playing the continual game of poker, or the 3 Michelin Stars Project. There is an eclectic in John, as evidenced in his piece on Project Managers are Anarchists and Punk Rockers.

Don't expect some long, dry, systematic treatise here. Instead, prepare for a pleasant whack or two.

Patrick Mayfield,

Author of *Practical People Engagement* & *Leading Yourself.*

Thank you Sarah for your encouragement and patience.

For Clementine, Dominic and Eloise who I am very proud of.

Contents

1. Introduction 14
2. Acknowledgements 16
3. Communication..18
4. A 'Lipsmackin' Communication Strategy 19
5. Article 19: Freedom of Expression 21
6. Henry V and Shakespeare's English 23
7. The word 'meeting'..25
8. Project communication and Transport for London 27
9. Communicate, Motivate, Collaborate 30
10. Competence & Knowledge Definitions 32
11. Marriages may come and go 33
12. Training: the wider context for delivering improvement ...35
13. Governance & Culture Definitions 38
14. Project Culture and the 'Tone from the Top'.......................39
15. The Scapegoat 42
16. Motivation Definition..45
17. A tale of two cities, a tale of two projects 46
18. The Blues Brothers 48
19. Why be a project professional?...50
20. It takes courage to stand alone...52
21. Master of Photography and Banal.......................................55
22. Newton's Laws of Motion and project momentum.............57
23. James Brown & seeing the light with QUBE 60
24. Interpersonal Skills Definition..62
25. Guilty of Crimes against Creativity 63
26. Fight Director or Peacemaker 67
27. The People versus Precision 69
28. There is a lot of washing-up in the sink 74

29. Integrity and Reliability Definition....................................77
30. Project Manager – Sleepless in Peckham............................79
31. The Good Project Samaritan...81
32. Planning Definition..83
33. Heaven can wait, playing to the whistle............................84
34. The Richter Scale & seismic impact of a day of work.........86
35. Project Managers are Anarchists & Punk Rockers 91
36. Risk Definition 96
37. Risk, Captain Kirk, and Good Governance.........................97
38. If it looks like a duck..99
39. Miscellaneous 103
40. The laws of the game...104
41. User stories and Business Intelligence 106
42. Art is never finished, only abandoned...............................109
43. 3 Michelin Stars Projects 111
44. Business Case Definition 114
45. Monet, Impressionism & project investment appraisal ...115
46. Acres of Diamonds & Business Intelligence......................118
47. References..120
48. Index 135

John Chapman, MIoD, MAPM, MISM, BSc (Hons)
John Chapman is Programme Director for TouchstoneFMS (www.touchstonefms.co.uk). His first experience of IT solutions was in the early 1980's working on an ICL ME29 mainframe. Since then he has run a software development team developing programs in the late 1980s and early 1990s on UNIX using Informix 4GL, then moving into project management and programme management.

From a business solutions perspective his experience includes implementing financial and management accounting solutions, spend control and document management solutions, business intelligence solutions, CRM solutions and leading programmes of business change.

With over 30 years of experience, including international programmes and projects, with the logistical and culture challenges they bring, he has very relevant practical on the ground experience. This is supported by a strong academic understanding of the subject of Programme and Project management.

He authored:

- Kafka, Pulp Fiction, Beer and Projects (available in printed and kindle format)
- Project and Programme accounting: a Practical Guide for Professional Services Organisations and IT

He was a member of the authoring group of the Gower Handbook of Programme Management 1st edition; an acknowledged contributor to Managing Successful Programmes, 1st Edition, and an acknowledged contributor to APM Introduction to Programme Management 1st edition.

John is an active member of the Association for Project Management Specific Interest Group on Programme Management (www.apm.org.uk/progm), and regularly speaks on the subject of Programme and Project Management.

His professional qualifications are a Member of the Institute of Directors (MIoD), a Member of the Association for Project Management, (MAPM), and a Master of the Institute of Sales Management (MISM).

His blogs are regularly published at

- www.TouchstoneFMS.co.uk
- www.TouchstoneBI.co.uk
- www.TouchstoneSpendManagement.co.uk
- www.apm.org.uk*

His personal interests include photography and art.

* The Association for Project Management. The Chartered Body for the Project Profession with over 23,000 individual members.

1. Introduction

There is a well-known WWI poster of Lord Kitchener pointing his finger with the words below saying

'Wants You'. Join Your Country's Army'.

This was a call to arms for the people of Great Britain to engage in the war effort.

Projects can be a battle at times. There are finite resources available, multiple projects running at the same time with varying priorities, and business as usual constraints. Technically we can produce Gantt Charts, Risk Registers, Communication Strategies, Ad Hoc Reports, Red Amber Green Indicators and so forth. These will not get the work done.

The project manager needs to go out and cajole, encourage, motivate, flatter, coax, persuade and sweet-talk the team to make progress.

To do so requires communication and motivation. There are two sides to a communication, the sender and the receiver. It is the responsibility of the sender to ensure the message is clear and understood. If the message is clear, and it is motivating, the team will be more likely to work on our project than another.

Yet how is such a thing achieved? One way is by looking at a broader spectrum. If we appeal to individuals based on their own interests and relate it to terms they understand, the willingness to learn and comprehension is considerably improved.

Consider the film The Full Monty. The motivator was the money received from the sale of tickets for putting on the show. As an unemployed group of people, extra cash in the pocket would be very welcome. Yet the group needed to dance and this was a challenge until one of them sees the link between Dancing and Football.

It's the Arsenal offside trap, int' it?

- You what?

- The Arsenal offside trap.

Lomper here is Tony Adams, right?

Any bugger looks like scoring,...

..we all step forward in a line

and wave our arms around like a fairy.

That's easy[1].

Learning dance moves was difficult, relate it to football and it is became easier.

Conclusion

The book is divided into sections based on a number of themes, communication, culture, motivation, people skills, and so forth. Within each are one or more blogs that seek to relate project work to the wider world: to make it more interesting, more acceptable, more understandable.

From this to engage with our colleagues so they appreciate it is their individual input which is needed for a successful project.

John Chapman

2. Acknowledgements

My thanks to my colleagues at TouchstoneFMS, in particular to Keith Birch and David Birch for their encouragement; to Stephanie Dean who provides feedback on my blogs, together with publishing them on the Touchstone Web Sites; to Joanne Henson who has a passion for writing and publishing; to Denise Neary whose design advice is always valuable, and to everyone in the respective divisions of:

- TouchstoneFMS:
  www.TouchstoneFMS.co.uk

- Touchstone Spend Management:
  www.TouchstoneSpendManagement.co.uk

- Touchstone Business Intelligence:
  www.TouchstoneBI.co.uk

- Touchstone Energy:
  www.TouchstoneEnergy.co.uk

- Touchstone CRM:
  www.TouchstoneCRM.co.uk

Being an active Member of the Association for Project Management has introduced me to many thought leaders and thinkers. In my book 'Kafka, Pulp Fiction, Beer and Projects' I thanked many of them and do so again.

For this publication I also send my appreciation to Dr. Jon Broome, Dr. James Dale, Martin Samphire, Merv Wyeth, Patrick Mayfield, Ricardo Vargas and Dr Ed Wallington.

Thank you also to Kirsten Bird at the Association for Project Management who publishes my blogs and provides valuable feedback on the content.

In the wider project community thank you to Paul Hodgkins, Eddie Obeng, Reinhard Wagner, Farhad Abdollahyan and Jonathan Norman. Their ideas, thought leadership and passion for programme and project management is an inspiration.

Finally to those individuals who I will meet and work with in programmes and projects yet to start, I look forward to working with you to deliver successful outcomes.

3. Communication

Communication[2]

Communication is the means by which information or instructions are exchanged. Successful communication occurs when received meaning is the same as the transmitted meaning.

Personal Communication[3]

Personal communication describes the essential aspects of effective communication. Both the content and the means of communication (tone of voice, channel and amount of information) have to be clear and appropriate for the target audience

4. A 'Lipsmackin' Communication Strategy

> Lipsmackin' thirstquenchin' acetastin' motivatin' goodbuzzin' cooltalkin' highwalkin' fastlivin' evergivin' coolfizzin' Pepsi[4].

Is from an advert of the 1970's promoting Pepsi Cola explaining 10 things Pepsi Cola does.

At project initiation I am often asked why we need to develop a Communication Strategy. Consider the following 52 different ways to communicate (as of November 2016)

Work email, Gmail, Outlook.com, Yahoo! Mail, snail mail, courier, WhatsApp, Snapchat, Facebook, Facebook Messenger, Instagram, Skype, WebEx, Facetime, landline audio, personal mobile phone, work mobile phone, text message, iMessage, picture message, video message, voice mail message, conference calls, face to face meetings, town hall meetings, stand up meetings, sit down meetings, meetings in the corridor, water cooler meetings, project reports, posters, flyers, handouts, brochures, pamphlets, booklets, newsletters, bulletins, YouTube, Dailymotion, Vimeo, Yammer, websites, SharePoint, Google Docs, Google Sheets, OneNote, wikis, LinkedIn, Xing, Tumblr and digital signage.

The success of a project ultimately relies on those who will be using the solution. They need to be properly engaged and informed.

So that why it's best to discuss how to effectively communicate, and why we need to agree a Lipsmackin' Communication Strategy at project initiation.

5. Article 19: Freedom of Expression

The Universal Declaration of Human Rights (UDHR)[5] is a declaration adopted by the United Nations General Assembly on 10 December 1948 at the Palais de Chaillot, Paris.

The Declaration arose directly from the experience of the Second World War and represents the first global expression of what many people believe to be the rights to which all human beings are inherently entitled.

Article 19 of the UDHR[6] says

> *Everyone has the right to freedom of opinion and expression; this right includes freedom to hold opinions without interference and to seek, receive and impart information and ideas through any media and regardless of frontiers.*

When we are designing a solution to a business problem we need open dialogue, discussion of the business need and 'freedom of opinion and expression'. This is easier said than done.

In a workshop environment it might not be possible, for individuals are fearful of political backlash. There may be dominant characters whose approach is confrontational and aggressive, who will shout down other ideas and opinions. Alternatively the group could contain a number of introverts, individuals who are shy and reticent. They may well have much to offer in terms of systems design, yet will not contribute in an open forum.

In the Art of War, Sun Tzu said 'Supreme excellence consists in breaking the enemy's resistance without fighting'. Instead of going into battle with dominant individuals, or seeking to extract information from an introvert in an open session, we need to find a way of working with them.

Alternatives to open workshops could be one to one interviews, small focus groups, conversations using the Chatham House Rule[7], subjects-in-tandem, surveys and questionnaires, work sampling and so forth. In doing so we are able to provide an opportunity for 'freedom of opinion and expression' irrespective of the types of character involved.

6. Henry V and Shakespeare's English

What if we wrote our executive summary in Shakespeare's English?

The text below is taken from an Executive summary of a business case justifying the implementation of the spend control solution Proactis. It has been converted into Shakespeare's English[8].

The client hast did identify the needeth f'r a spendeth control solution and the Proactis solution hast been evaluat'd during a number of presentations. Proactis is the market leading solution and whilst independent of the finance solution, Microsoft holp fund the development of an integration bridge between Proactis & Dynamics GP (the finance application hath used by the client f'r many years), indicating Microsoft's recognition of the importance of Proactis to fulfil spendeth control requirements.

Proactis is fully web-based, offering the client the opportunity to maketh the entire process from charge requisition to invoice payment much moo efficient whilst eke eliminating excessive pap'r flow. one key area whither these efficiencies can beest seen early into the roll-out is the ability f'r users to approve invoices only by exception. coequal those invoices requiring final approval art did manage electronically offering the end-user full visibility of the purchase history and audit trail on-line simplifying the process greatly.

Having did identify Proactis as a valorous fit f'r the client, a short project hast been undertaken to buildeth the business case and confirm the feasibility of implementing Proactis.

There is much to be learned from Shakespeare's use of language. An original sentence starting 'Having identified Proactis as a good fit for the client' is now converted to 'Having did identify Proactis as a valorous fit f'r the client'.

The Thesaurus in MS Word suggested instead of valorous words such as 'noble, intrepid, courageous, heroic, gallant, fearless'.

For our future documentation, let us bring life to the words as Shakespeare did.

> *For Proactis is a noble fit, delivered by a courageous group of gallant and honourable folk, who will deliver considerable benefit to you and your good people.*
>
> *And gentlemen in England now a-bed, Shall think themselves accursed they were not here*[9]*, to deliver the Proactis with good cheer.*

7. The word 'meeting'

Definition

On typing into Google[10] 'the definition of meeting' it provides the answers

1. an assembly of people for a particular purpose, especially for formal discussion
2. a situation when two or more people meet, by chance or arrangement

In business the term is used very generically. Yet is this just laziness?

Synonyms

The synonyms Google quotes include:

> gathering, assembly, conference, congregation, convention, summit, forum, convocation, conclave, council of war; caucus; consultation, audience, interview, encounter, contact, introduction, appointment, assignation, rendezvous, tweetup, tryst.

Microsoft Word thesaurus also offers up for the word meeting

> seminar, consultation, Get-together, gathering, reunion, gathering, appointment, engagement, discussion, seminar

A total of 32 different terms to use instead of meeting.

Are you thinking so what?

Semantics are important. Instead of saying 'We will have a meeting', let us use the richness of the English language to propose

- We will have a consultation
- We will have a discussion
- We will have a seminar
- We will have an argument
- We will have a get-together
- We will have a planning council

Something with more substance than just saying the word 'meeting'. It will focus the mind on what the purpose is, and move away from the mundane 'I am in a meeting'.

8. Project communication and Transport for London

Travel on a Transport for London Metropolitan line train to learn about how to effectively communicate. Prior to getting on the train look around the platform. There will be a Transport for London (TFL) Tube Map showing the full extent of the London Underground Network. Above the platform, a dot matrix indicator will show the next one, two or three trains, the number of minutes to wait before their expected arrival and the train's ultimate destination. During peak times, a member of TFL staff will announce the arrival of the train and advise when it is to depart and the doors closing.

On joining the train you will see maps of the line, and as the train goes on its journey there are audio announcements of the next station to be arrived at. On arrival there is an announcement at the station of its name, together with the ultimate destination of the train. If the train is stopping at an interchange with other lines or a mainline station further information is given. A dot matrix indicator will also show the destination of the train and also the name of the next station. Should there be delays on the line, the train driver makes announcements to keep the passengers informed.

The web site, www.tfl.gov.uk, has a journey planner and up to date information about the status of the individual train lines. TFL also provide the ability to subscribe for mobile text alerts as to delays on your journey to and from work.

So what can we learn from Transport for London for our project communication strategy?

1. Who are we communicating to?
    a. Those inside the project team
    b. Those directly affected by the project
    c. Interested parties
    d. External stakeholders

2. What do we need to communicate?
    a. The progress of the project
    b. The ultimate go live date
    c. The next key milestone dates
    d. Any deviations from the plan

3. How often to communicate?
    a. At project initiation
    b. Daily / weekly / monthly

4. What method of communication is required?
    a. Visual such as posters – important for those who are deaf or hard of hearing
    b. Audio announcements – important for those who are blind or partially sighted
    c. Web sites
    d. Text alerts
    e. Town hall meetings

5. Where does the communication need to be located?
    a. In the office
    b. On a web site
    c. Available on the mobile phone
    d. By email

6. What resources are required to deliver the communication?
    a. Project manager
    b. Project team
    c. External individuals

Six simple questions to answer.

9. Communicate, Motivate, Collaborate

The Pilot's Mantra

Airline pilots are taught the mantra 'Aviate, Navigate, Communicate'[11]. It stands to reason that they are there first and foremost to fly the plane and keep it in the air. Secondly, they need to navigate the plane to the target destination, and then to communicate with those who need to know what the status is, how the flight is progressing, any issues and so forth. For those interested in the eloquence of this, three is the magic number of literary composition[12].

The Project Manager's Mantra

Now what about when it comes to project work? I suggest an alternative mantra:

'Communicate, Motivate, Collaborate'

The first thing to do is to C*ommunicate*. Project planning requires communication, risk management requires communication, issue resolution requires communication, stakeholder management requires communication. As project managers it can't be denied that excellent communication skills are essential and we must use them.

Next the team needs to be *Motivated*, to have drive and determination. If they do not have fire in their belly, it needs to be lit. John Kotter says 'Establishing a sense of urgency is crucial to gaining needed co-operation'[13]. Let us inspire, encourage, embolden, and fire up the team to deliver.

Collaborate means to work together. Having communicated what needs to be done, motivated the team with the desire to deliver, we collaborate together, to complete the work successfully.

Conclusion: three powerful words

Pilots

Aviate, Navigate, Communicate,

Project managers

Communicate, Motivate, Collaborate

10. Competence & Knowledge Definitions

Individual Competence Development[14]

Motivation theory and current research results show that individuals strive to develop their competences in order to perform better in their current position, to get more and more interesting tasks and to enhance their career opportunities. Project, programme or portfolio – related work is based on collaboration with team members from all kinds of disciplines, internal and external parties (such as clients and suppliers), and therefore competence development happens in such collective settings. Project experience adds to the competence of every individual and also to the teams and organisations as social systems.

Knowledge[15]

Knowledge is the essential element for the creation of successful physical and virtual products and services. It can be viewed as an organized set of content, skills, and capabilities gained through experience as well as through formal and informal learning that organizations and practitioners apply to make sense of new and existing data and information. It can also exist as previously analyzed and formatted lessons and stories that are already adaptable to new situations.

11. Marriages may come and go

Marriages may come and go, but the game must go on.

Felix Unger, The Odd Couple

These immortal words, from the film The Odd Couple[16], are in reference to the game of poker. For those of you who play poker you will have heard of the concept of the continual game. The game never ends, we are merely players who join and leave at different points in our lives. It is not a new game, it is a learning experience with different players. The rules remain the same. The opportunity is there to win or to lose. How well we play is up to us.

Project work is the same. Individual projects may have a start and end. Yet those working in the field of programme and project management will understand that this is a continuum. The start of a project may be new to some, yet for us it is an introduction into that game, the great project game. Around the table are the players. We bring our experience, our knowledge, our mental game, our intellect. Project initiation should enlighten us to who is involved, what are the stakes, the rewards, the risks, the costs of failure.

The project is in progress and there are problems: in poker there are bad beats. Those times when the cards turn against us. Do we fold, walk away like a spoilt child in anger, throw our toys out the pram? A good player recognises a bad beat when it happens and deals with it. Keep playing quality poker.

In projects there are times when the Black Swan events occur[17]. Those unexpected things that could not have been predicted. The project is brought to a halt, the team get panicked, the project executive is worried. What do we do? We continue to be professional, to play the highest quality project game. Panic and the hole gets deeper. Stand back and reflect, regroup, re-motivate, regain trust, restart, and the journey continues.

It is mental strength that is required, a strength of character to keep going. Epictus said

> 'Circumstances don't make a man, they only reveal him to himself'.

What will we learn during that project about our fellow players? They come from a spectrum starting with the strong, those we can rely on, in who we can trust; the weaker players who need support in times of trouble; and at the other end, aggressive confrontational individuals who are trying to hide their insecurities.

Experienced poker players will see them around the table. Project professionals will have encountered them in the project team. Irrespective of where they are, our responsibility is to continue promoting the highest level of professionalism. Keep playing a good game, and when the next project (game) comes along, to join bringing our improved skills and experience to the table.

12. Training: the wider context for delivering improvement

It's important when creating a training programme to consider the organisation's strategy for improving employee skills and capabilities.

For example when looking at software training you can look at the required skills from two perspectives:

- The first relates to the software functionality, and how to effectively use the software solution that is being implemented.
- The second, and most importantly, is to recognise that the software is used as part of a wider organisational objective to improve operational efficiency and effectiveness. The individual's role in the organisation does not sit in isolation. The software is an enabling tool and the training needs to focus on the wider context, the bigger picture

I'll use a real-world example, which is Supplier Engagement and Supplier Relationship Management (SRM). It is part of the Proactis solution that we deliver and it provides information about the organisation's supplier base.

In engaging with the suppliers there are skills required to develop effective relationships. Beyond training on the software itself, there also needs to be training on working with suppliers including collaboration, joint ways of working and how to improve co-operation.

When recommending training approaches, the train-the-trainer proves to be cost effective. It is there to equip key individuals, who are likely to be subject matter experts in the role, to understand the implications of the software solution. They are then able to provide an enhanced level of training to the end users, covering both the software functionality (which an application trainer would give), and the contextual content relating to the organisation's current and future business processes.

The location of the training again is context specific. One-on-one training might be best at the person's desk, using their own work as relevant and applicable examples. Classroom style training, where there are groups of up to eight people who need to be brought together into a single location, is the traditional method that is thought of when referring to training.

More recently the use of social media and other technologies have enabled training to move to more of a 'self serve' approach. Recording webinars, screen shots with voice overs and posting these on intranets, extranets, YouTube and other such sites allows for cost effective distribution of learning material. There is still a place for printed material, whether this is one page handouts, printed manuals, or a combination of the two.

In my experience, early on in the project the training strategy has to be prepared and agreed. This will cover who needs to be trained, what are their current skill sets, what future skills do they need, where are they located (to understand geographical considerations), what type of training might work best for them (self learning, one-on-one, classroom) and who is to give the training.

By considering training in this wider context of the overall organisational objectives, we can raise the operational efficiency and effectiveness – using the project as the mechanism for managing and delivering this improvement.

13. Governance & Culture Definitions

Governance[18]

Governance relates to the set of policies, regulations, functions, processes, procedures and responsibilities that define the establishment, management and control of projects, programmes and portfolios

Culture[19]

Culture in a corporate context can be defined as a combination of the values, attitudes and behaviours manifested by a company in its operations and relations with its stakeholders. These stakeholders include shareholders, employees, customers, suppliers and the wider community and environment which are affected by a company's conduct

14. Project Culture and the 'Tone from the Top'

In July 2016 the Financial Reporting Council (FRC) published 'Corporate Culture and the Role of Boards[20]'.

In the Executive Summary it notes:

> *Culture in a corporate context can be defined as a combination of the values, attitudes and behaviours manifested by a company in its operations and relations with its stakeholders. These stakeholders include shareholders, employees, customers, suppliers and the wider community and environment which are affected by a company's conduct*

The report references the UK Corporate Governance Code[21] which states:

> *One of the key roles for the board includes establishing the culture, values and ethics of the company. It is important that the board sets the correct "tone from the top". The directors should lead by example and ensure that good standards of behaviour permeate throughout all levels of the organisation.*

Project Governance & Culture

Project Governance is a subset of Corporate Governance. The Project Board will need to consider the culture of the project. What is the 'tone from the top' of the Project to those individuals who are in the project team, and the wider community who are affected by the project outcomes?

In the delivery of business solutions we need to encourage open dialogue. This starts pre-project with the preparation of the business case. What are the benefits required to be delivered? Where are there organisation issues that need addressing? Does the organisational culture need to change?

During project delivery there will be design discussions and development of business process changes. Each one to be considered and probed in depth. Consultation, cross hierarchy process reviews[22] and debate are important to look at the bigger picture.

User Acceptance testing should involve a representative set of individuals, who can provide open feedback on what is encountered. On go live, issues identified need to be fed back quickly and managed.

Conclusion

Culture is much more about people than it is about rules. Codes of conduct are a baseline; a culture is created by what you do rather than what you say. 'The alignment and consistency of behaviours of leaders, and how they communicate through words and actions is the essential starting point'[23].

What is the 'tone from the top' that will be set for your project?

For business solutions projects it needs to be one of open dialogue, leadership during delivery, and recognition that everyone has a contribution to make.

15. The Scapegoat

'The Scapegoat is a painting by William Holman Hunt which depicts the 'scapegoat' described in the book of Leviticus'[24].

At a project initiation meeting one of the first slides I presented had a picture of this painting. The purpose was to explain that if you want blame someone then it is this goat, otherwise it is your responsibility to deliver or advise what is preventing you from working. There will be no finger pointing or blaming of others. We are professionals and should work in a responsible way[25].

As a manager it is our duty to bring together the team and give them the skills and the opportunity to deliver. If there are obstacles preventing this, to see how these can be moved.

Yet what if an organisation has a culture of blaming others, of picking on those who are seen to be weaker, and management not dealing with this? Well why not create a specific job of Scape Goat?

Job Description: Scape-goat

Job Brief

We are looking for a particular type of person. This individual will be employed on the project to take the blame for the wrongdoings, mistakes, or faults of others. On every project there are those individuals who will find excuses for not getting work done. For reasons of expediency, and to avoid management having to deal with those suffering from laziness, torpor, lethargy, indolence, slothfulness or excusitus[26], this role has been created. You might also be referred to as the whipping boy where you will be held responsible for the incompetence, ineffectiveness, stupidity and uselessness of others.

Responsibilities

- To take the blame
- To apologise for the incompetence and indifference of others
- To identify failings in the project and make it look as if it was your fault
- To be available at all times of day or night to pick up the phone to ask for forgiveness.
- To be contrite
- To be apologetic
- To be remorseful
- To be sorry
- To show penitence

Skills

The scope of this role is not limited to project work. Whilst at the company you will also be blamed for poor sales performance, the missing of sales targets, lousy customer service, and the incompetence of management.

Reporting to

You will have no line manager for they cannot be held responsible for your actions. This is a standalone role.

Conclusion

Project are challenging. A blame culture and finger pointing does not work. It is destructive and demotivating. Projects require a team of people who will work together and can depend on each other.

At project initiation we need to emphasise the importance of having a cohesive group who are there to deliver and be successful. A group who know and can see they have the visible support of the senior management.

16. Motivation Definition

Motivation[27]

To get optimal team performance it is crucial to understand the motivation of team members. To get there the individual has to spend time with people in order to understand who they are and what makes them tick. The individual should keep in mind that values, experiences and goals of others might be very different from his or her own.

17. A tale of two cities, a tale of two projects

It was the best of times,	it was the worst of times,
it was the age of wisdom,	it was the age of foolishness,
it was the epoch of belief,	it was the epoch of incredulity,
it was the season of Light,	it was the season of Darkness
it was the spring of hope,	it was the winter of despair,
we had everything before us,	we had nothing before us,
we were all going direct to Heaven,	we were all going direct the other way

Charles Dickens wrote these words in A Tale of Two Cities (1859). '.. it tells the story of two men, Charles Darnay and Sydney Carton, who look similar but are very different in traits[28].

As we approach a new project how do we view the challenge ahead? What are the traits that we bring?

A positive outlook, seeing light, hope, and belief in our abilities to deliver	It is doom, gloom and negativity. There is no hope and no ability.
The opportunities are endless.	We don't have the time or the inclination to look for opportunities
There is the prospect to bring in new ways of working: to remove the mundane, the monotony and replace it with something interesting and stimulating.	New ways of working never worked before. The team are lazy and only deserve mundane work. No point in trying to make it interesting
In working with our colleagues, we will develop our skills in people management, empathy and understanding. Inclusion, discussion and consultation is the new way.	Indifference, intolerance, apathy and lethargy persist. The intimidators, oppressors and aggressive ones will not change.
The project journey may be a challenging one, yet it is worth it.	Don't waste my time.

18. The Blues Brothers

'The Blues Brothers[29] is a 1980 American musical crime comedy film directed by John Landis. It stars John Belushi and Dan Aykroyd as "Joliet" Jake and Elwood Blues. The story is a tale of redemption for paroled convict Jake and his brother Elwood, who set out on "a mission from God" to save from foreclosure the Catholic orphanage in which they were raised'

Jake and Elwood Blues go to the Triple Rock Baptist Church where they hear the Revered Cleophus James (played by James Brown) preaching. The Reverend is an inspirational and motivational speaker, raising the energy levels of the congregation who commence dancing, singing and running around the church almost to fever pitch, praising the Lord.

It is during this sermon that Jake has an epiphany realising the way to save the orphanage is to re-form the band. They are then on a 'mission from God' and nothing will stop them.

The International Project Management Association publish an Individual Competence Baseline (ICB)[30], currently in its fourth edition.

Section 4.4.4 of the ICB is Relationships and Engagement.

> *'The Purpose of this competence element is to enable the individual to build and maintain relationships and to understand that the ability to engage with others is a precondition for collaboration, commitment and ultimately performance'.*

On reading this can sound a little dry and uninspiring. However it just needs a little interpretation.

James Brown was only in the film for a few minutes. Yet it was his motivational speaking, his energy and repetition of the words 'Do you see the light?' that inspired the epiphany in Jake. Once engaged Jake and Elwood were committed to deliver.

So for your next project consider how will you engage with your team 'to see the light' and commit them to high performance, irrespective of the obstacles ahead.

19. Why be a project professional?

A question asked by those thinking of coming into the profession.

Programmes and projects are not easy. They are challenging endeavours requiring determination, tenacity, drive, energy, a range of technical skills, people skills, subject matter expertise, and so the list goes on. We must ask 'Is there something more to consider?'

'George Herbert Leigh Mallory (18 June 1886 – 8 or 9 June 1924) was an English mountaineer who took part in the first three British expeditions to Mount Everest in the early 1920s[31]'. In his book Climbing Everest: The Complete Writings of George Mallory, he writes[32]:

> *"How to get the best of it all? One must conquer, achieve, get to the top; one must know the end to be convinced that one can win the end - to know there's no dream that mustn't be dared. . . Is this the summit, crowning the day? How cool and quiet! We're not exultant; but delighted, joyful; soberly astonished. . . Have we vanquished an enemy? None but ourselves. Have we gained success? That word means nothing here. Have we won a kingdom? No. . . and yes. We have achieved an ultimate satisfaction. . . fulfilled a destiny. . . To struggle and to understand - never this last without the other; such is the law. . ."*

So why be a project professional?

George Mallory said

> 'It is not the mountain we conquer, but ourselves'.

Consider your programme, your project, as your mountain to be conquered and

> 'to be convinced that one can win'.

20. It takes courage to stand alone

"Throughout the centuries there were men who took first steps down new roads armed with nothing but their own vision. Their goals differed, but they all had this in common: that the step was first, the road new, the vision unborrowed, and the response they received — hatred.

The great creators — the thinkers, the artists, the scientists, the inventors — stood alone against the men of their time.

Every great new thought was opposed. Every great new invention was denounced. The first motor was considered foolish. The airplane was considered impossible. The power loom was considered vicious. Anaesthesia was considered sinful. But the men of unborrowed vision went ahead. They fought, they suffered and they paid. But they won."

Ayn Rand, The Fountainhead[33]

Projects and programmes involve creating something new. It may require pushing back the boundaries of thinking, to stretch the imagination, to challenge current methods and best practice, to change behaviours. We need to remember the words of Ayn Rand when we commence our journey.

It takes courage to stand alone, against a tide of negativity and denouncement.

To help overcome this we put together a Project Structure. The PRINCE2 Project Board consists of a series of roles, Executive, Senior User, Senior Supplier. According to the PRINCE2 Manual 'The Executive, supported by the Project Manager, is responsible for agreeing a suitable team structure and tailoring it to the project's size, risk and complexity'[34].

We make recommendations on a Project Board structure based on the business systems areas being affected by the Project. For example an implementation of the finance system would include

- Project Executive: The Finance Director or Chief Finance Officer
- Senior Users: The Financial Controller, The Head of IT
- Senior Supplier: TouchstoneFMS

For a Spend Control only project covering purchase to pay:

- Project Executive: Head of Purchasing / Head of Procurement
- Senior Users
    - Purchasing manager
    - Financial Controller / Accounts Payable manager
    - The Head of IT

Senior Supplier: TouchstoneFMS

Selection of the respective Project Board members requires the identification of those with sufficient seniority to take decisions, understand the business area being changed, appreciate the contents of the project business case and can defend the project.

This last item, defence of the project is important. All members of the project team are there to defend the project; the customer and the supplier are on the same team, working together to realise their respective business cases. Each supporting the other to deliver the required output or outcome. So at the end, others will look back and say

> *They fought, they suffered and they paid. But they won.*

21. Master of Photography and Banal

The Master of Photography is a TV series showing on Sky TV[35], There are a number of contestants who compete for a winning prize of €150,000. The challenge each week is to take photos based on a theme. During an episode, Oliviero Toscani, who is one of the judges, critiqued a photo and said it was banal. A review of the thesaurus in MS Word gives alternatives to banal of commonplace, trite, hackneyed, predictable, facile, trivial to name a few.

Projects can be of a similar nature such as an upgrade to a finance system, a new implementation of a spend control solution, a revision to the chart of accounts to improve reporting. At first sight they look the same as previous projects. The software solution and version has been implemented many times; the design of the chart of accounts means having a design workshop, a reporting review, data migration assessment, configuration and testing. There is a focus on getting things done quickly, reducing the time to go live. Every cost estimate is reviewed carefully and questioned. 'Can you do things quicker? we are asked. By using previously prepared documentation this does reduce the level of rework. Meeting agendas, masterclass definitions, common work breakdown structures do have their place.

Yet the danger is that it ends up as colours by numbers, a banal project.

We must remember that projects are about people. The people will be different. Their environment has its own esoteric issues to consider. There may be cultural implications, governance structures that look the same but are not, political issues to uncover. The training could range from insignificant to an all-encompassing approach including providing skills outside of the software functionality.

Our challenge is to take each project as a unique, innovative, pioneering original event; to be creative in the way that we approach the project, the people, the environment. Certainly we bring to the table previous lessons learned, and they may have been learnt the hard way. However what did not work elsewhere does not mean it should be discounted before at least some initial discussion.

It will be harder work mentally as assumptions are challenged, areas are probed and questioned. Yet the end result should be something we are proud to put our name to.

What do we choose, Banal or Creative?

22. Newton's Laws of Motion and project momentum

Newton's First Law of Motion states that "every object in a state of uniform motion tends to remain in that state of motion unless an external force is applied to it[36]

Consequently

An object that is at rest will stay at rest unless a force acts upon it.

An object that is in motion will not change its velocity unless a force acts upon it[37].

Projects

Deriving from Newton's First Law of Motion, we can state:

An individual that is at rest will stay at rest unless a force acts upon it.

An individual that is in motion will not change its velocity unless a force acts upon it.

The purpose of the project is to produce change. The purpose of the programme is to realise outcomes. To realise these we need to bring a force to bear on the individual / the organisation. How much force is required? This is where Newton's Second law of motion applies.

Newton's Second Law of Motion

We want to bring about change, a change in behaviours, a change in working practices, a change in direction. According to Newton's second law of motion we need to bring a net force to deliver this change. The larger the mass (i.e. the larger the organisation) the more force is required. The bigger the change in direction may require more than one force to be applied. Once the change has commenced the force needs to be maintained otherwise momentum is lost, or increase the force to increase acceleration.

Conclusion

How to bring about this force? John Kotter identifies an 8 step process for leading change[38].

1. Create: Sense of Urgency

2. Build: Guiding Coalition

3. Form: Strategic Vision & Initiatives

4. Enlist: Volunteer Army

5. Enable: Action by removing barriers

6. Generate: Short term wins

7. Sustain: Acceleration

8. Institute: Change

People are not machines. They can be irrational and behave in ways that appear illogical.

Whatever the force is that prevents momentum (e.g. inertia, indolence, apathy, lethargy, laziness, torpor), remember Sir Isaac Newton's classical mechanics, a force needs to be applied. John Kotter gives us eight steps to follow to apply this force.

23. James Brown & seeing the light with QUBE

> Do you see the light?
>
> Do you see the light?
>
> Have you seen the light?
>
> *James Brown as Reverend Cleophus James*[39]

In January 2017 I was invited to join one of Eddie Obeng's Pentacle[40] Presentations using the QUBE[41] virtual solution. In advance of the presentation time was spent learning how to navigate the software and on the day in question I duly connected in. My thoughts were that this was to be another Webinar type presentation, a few polls, interaction using a chat box, and at the end the presentation made available as a recorded session.

How wrong could I be? The QUBE Learn + Do Ware opened my eyes to the opportunities to have meaningful discussions in a virtual environment. The ability to 'sit round a table' and have conversations with individuals who have connected across the world was engaging. Joining white board sessions to share thoughts such as 'Hopes and Fears' using virtual Post-It notes, brought life to the warm up before a presentation. During the presentation there were breakout sessions where particular items could be discussed, and feedback then provided to the presenter.

February 2017 and Eddie had invited me to run a session. The subject being the alignment of Social Media with project and programme management. I had given this presentation on a number of occasions, yet this was to be different. No more talking through a series of PowerPoint slide. Instead QUBE was there to enable an engagement with the audience. Questions can be asked of them, and of me; points of clarification sought. Part of the presentation was about the importance of speaking clearly. We were able to practice together vocal warm up exercises. One of the attendees explained that they used QUBE to develop documentation. Virtual sessions replaced the reliance on email and travel to meet people. Documentation was prepared interactively which overcame the issues of configuration management and version control, of getting items read and reviewed.

Interaction, communication, sharing of ideas, white boards, post it notes, presentations, breakout areas, communication across the world. Prior to joining the session in January, like Jake Blues, I was sceptical. January the light shone on me, February and I had 'seen the light'.

In the film the Blues Brothers, James Brown is asking the question 'Do you see the light?' The light has turned on in my mind the potential of QUBE Learn + Do Ware and virtual environments. The next challenge is to bring this epiphany to a wider community.

24. Interpersonal Skills Definition

Interpersonal Skills[42]

Interpersonal skills are the means by which people relate to, and interact with, other people.

25. Guilty of Crimes against Creativity

Anger and aggression sometimes seem to be protective because they bring energy to bear on a particular situation, but that energy is blind. It takes a calm mind to be able to consider things from different angles and points of view.

Dalai Lama

Projects that are delivering new ways of working, new approaches to business process, looking at end to end systems thinking require creative thinking. To do this our team members need to be given the opportunity to reflect and consider, to work in an environment that encourages this.

'Teresa Amabile, a psychologist at the Harvard Business School, describes four "creativity killers", each of which constricts working memory, the mental space in which brainstorms occur and creating flourishes, and squelches risk taking"[43]:

- *Surveillance*: Hovering and constant scrutiny. This stifles the essential sense of freedom needed for creative thinking.

- *Evaluation*: A critical view that comes too soon or is too intense. Creative ideas should be critiqued – not all are equally good and promising ones can be refined and honed by helpful criticism – but evaluation is counterproductive when it leads to a preoccupation with being judged

- *Overcontrol*: Micromanaging every step of the way. Like surveillance, it fosters and oppressive sense of constriction which discourages originality.

- *Relentless Deadlines:* A too-intense schedule that creates panic. While some pressure can be motivating and deadlines and goals can focus attention, they can kill the fertile "off time" where fresh ideas flourish'.

Consider the projects and environments you have worked in. Have you encountered one or more of these creativity killers? For Project Managers how you could remove these?

- *Surveillance*: Management should be by exception. The parameters in which the project is running (time, cost, risk, quality, etc) are identified at the start of the project or the start of a Stage. Leave the team to work within these parameters.

- *Evaluation*; How do you evaluate work? Individuals have different styles and approaches. Those who are good at generating new ideas may prefer to work alone[44]. Perhaps they are introverted and find it difficult to present, in open forum. Those attending the review need to be aware of their own styles. Confrontational, in your face, aggressive characters may be best excluded. The review team made up of those who know how to evaluate constructively.

- *Overcontrol*: What is the reporting style that is requested? Is it daily reviews? Are you constantly asking for percentage complete, estimated days to complete, and an updated risk assessment? An end of week review might be better. Reviewing progress and then having the weekend to reflect allows the brain time to reflect over the following weekend. If the review is on a Monday morning, then individuals may spend the weekend worrying about what will be said. Creativity is further reduced.

- *Relentless Deadlines*: Projects are about deadlines. When do we start? When do we finish? How quickly can you get the work done? Can we start something else sooner? Can we bring forward the go live date? There might be a large white board with a countdown showing how many days to go? The watercooler talk, project reviews, and visual aids all focusing on the deadline. Agree with the team realistic deadlines, and then why not leave them to get on with the work?

Conclusion

A purely technical project, akin to painting by numbers, may not require much creativity. It does need a productive team, one who can be focussed on the task at hand. If they spend too much time worrying about what will be said, the timelines involved, then little or nothing will be achieved. Micromanagement, over-control, harsh evaluation, and relentless deadlines are all crimes against creativity.

Let us be innocent of these crimes and give our teams the opportunity to be creative, original, innovative, pioneering and inventive.

26. Fight Director or Peacemaker

> 'A fighting director is charged with mapping out and overseeing staged combat in a film, play or other performance. These directors, also known as fight directors or fight choreographers, are experts in making fighting look realistic while keeping it safe for the actors and other participants. As a result, they work with the production's director to ensure the best possible look to anything from a fistfight to a gun battle'[45]

Conflicts arise during project work. It could come in the form of simmering discontent between individuals from the past that have never gone away. Changes can bring uncertainty and job insecurity. Design workshops and open discussion about new ways of working can be difficult for those involved. Individuals who are not eloquent may find themselves at a disadvantage. Whatever it is, when conflict does arise it needs to be dealt with.

Project professionals need the skills to be able to deal with conflict and crisis. What skills are required is given in Section 4.4.7 of the IPMA Individual Competence Baseline[46]. It states the purpose as:

> *To enable the individual to take effective action when a crisis or clash of opposing interests / incompatible personalities occurs*

The description notes that

> *'The individual can use a variety of means for reacting to potential or actual conflict and crisis, for example collaboration, compromise, prevention, persuasion, escalation or the use of power'*

As Project professionals we are there to deal with conflict and crisis, not as Fight Directors to oversee and direct the ensuing battle, enticing as that may appear to be.

27. The People versus Precision

My plans are not working

Have you worked on a project where you produce a plan, issue it out, then little happens. So you revise the plan, put in more detail, clarify exact periods, start times and end times, specific individuals, with ever increasing levels of granularity, and still there is no progress? Yet the plan is detailed, precise, exact, meticulous, and particular.

Precision & Exactitude

We see all around us ever greater levels of precision. A mobile phone can now tell our exact location. My desk, which is located at TouchstoneFMS Ltd, Triton Square*, London is North 51 Degrees, 52 minutes 55.299 seconds, and West -0 degrees, 14 minutes 05.259 seconds[47].

Apps are available for tracking, for scheduling, to do lists, driving directions, travel alerts, banking for immediate access to the account balance, health and fitness showing distance, average pace, maximum pace, average speed, maximum speed, calories and so forth. The lists in the different App Stores appear to be endless. This technology can create a false sense of security; that we know where we are and where we are going.

* As of the time of writing this book

Project Management

A project plan, prepared in a tool like Microsoft project, has settings for start time, end time, hours in the day, and working days in the month. Durations can be entered in months, weeks, days, hours or minutes. The calendar can be configured as Gregorian, Hijri, or Thai Buddhist. Activities can be scheduled with successor and predecessors defined. The baseline set and the actual start and actual finish compared against the baseline. Resource assignments as full day or part of a day with % allocation. Today's activities pushed out by email, calendars updated automatically. Timesheets are completed and the actual time compared to the planned time.

For some projects, those akin to painting by numbers, this is appropriate. You follow a fixed routine, a set of activities one after the other. All the deliverables can be listed, the resources identified and the end goal defined. These projects appear to be easy. The methodology works so we convince ourselves it can be used elsewhere. Yet this is not the case.

Complexity

In project management there are different types of complexity[48], one of which is 'Socio Political'. This 'is about soft skills, relationships, personalities and behaviours that arise under stress. It's not obvious how to manage a group of clients and stakeholders who change their minds and who behave in infinitely complex ways, especially under pressure'[49].

Soft skills are the hardest skills.

Ever greater levels of detail in a plan, tracking of actual time, setting of constraints, defining deliverables like a Hayes Manual is not appropriate where there is Socio Political complexity. What is required are a different set of skills. There are the terms 'soft skills' and 'hard skills'. It is the soft skills that are the hardest skills to develop. They require emotional maturity, tolerance, an open mind, mental strength, and a willingness to listen.

What to do?

In the RICS publication Stakeholder Engagement there are ten key principles[50] each with suggestions on actions to take. Three are listed here as a start point to consider.

- Principle 1: Communicate. Investigate people's preferred method of communication ... and then adopt these accordingly.

- Principle 2: Consult Early and Often. Ask questions about who the stakeholders are and once these have been identified identify their objectives, success criteria, constraints ...

- Principle 3: Remember they're only human. It is important to operate with an awareness of human feelings and these feelings ... will usually determine the success or failure of the initiative.

Conclusion

'Treat people ... as unique human beings, irrational at times, emotional, forgetful, with their own agendas, power, and fears. These are people with whom you can, and sometimes should, have conversations with, who may pleasantly surprise you with their responses and ideas'[51].

Once you have communicated with them, listened, considered, and thought about how this works in the context of the project, then it is time to start planning.

28. There is a lot of washing-up in the sink

Arriving home from a busy day at work, I walk into the kitchen and see a lot of washing-up in the sink. There are dishes from last night's dinner, this morning's breakfast, lunchtime plates and numerous coffee cups.

A comment is made to my partner 'There is a lot of washing up in the sink. (For those who live with someone, this might be considered a provocative comment in the first instance)'.

This can elicit three responses.

- *The Parent response*: Yes I have been very busy today, can you help me with it

- *The Adult response*: I know, the prioritisation of the tasks at home, including baby feeding, washing clothes and shopping meant this had to wait

- *The Child response*: What do you mean there is a lot of washing-up in the sink? Do you not realise how busy I have been? Up early this morning, on my feet all day trying to keep everything under control, and on arriving home the best you can do is criticise the state of the house.

Eric Berne[52] identified these three ego states as Parent, Adult and Child.

In Project work, understanding the psychology of individuals is important. What we say can be interpreted in different ways. Consider the question 'Have you finished reviewing the design document?' Replies could vary:

- *The Parent response*: Not yet, business as usual priorities have taken precedence. I will complete the review in the next few days.

- *The Adult response*: Can you help me with some business as usual work, so I can free up time to complete the review of the document.

- *The Child response*: Don't you realise how hard I work. My manager expects so much of me. Customers are demanding more and more. I arrive early, leave late, my family do not see me, and all you are interested in is your design document.

Now we can respond in different ways.

- *The Parent response*: I understand that you are busy. Thank you for letting me know when it will be completed.

- *The Adult response*: I will arrange additional resources to back fill your role, so giving you more time to do the project work

- *The Child response*: You think you work hard, look at the hours I put in and I don't complain. Just get the documentation reviewed and shut up complaining.

Communication is a two-way process. There is the sender and the receiver. What was said might not be heard in the way that it is meant. A little understanding of psychology could help us frame an appropriate response. In this way we maintain the relationship and see off a potentially inflammatory situation.

29. Integrity and Reliability Definition

Integrity[53]

There needs to be a concerted effort to improve trust in the motivations and integrity of business. Rules and sanctions clearly have their place, but will not on their own deliver productive behaviours over the long-term.

Sir Winfried Bischoff

Chairman, Financial Reporting Council

Ethical Behaviour[54]

The Board needs to show it has zero risk appetite for poor ethical behaviour. This sends a clear signal. Turning a blind eye to dubious behaviour is very dangerous.

Sir Peter Gershon, Chairman

National Grid

Personal integrity and reliability[55]

Integrity and reliability are built on consistency of values, emotions, actions and outcomes by saying what you do and doing what you are saying. By using ethical standards and moral principles as a basis for actions and decisions and by taking responsibility for individual actions and decisions, confidence is enabled and promoted. The individual is a person to rely on.

30. Project Manager – Sleepless in Peckham

In the BBC Television series Only Fools and Horses, one of the lead characters, Rodney Trotter, finds out his biological father was a man called Robbie Robdal who his mother had an affair with. At the end of the episode, Sleepless in Peckham, Rodney asks his brother Derek if he is anything like his father, to which "Del replies firmly by saying that Robdal was "a womaniser, a home-breaker, a con-man, a thief, a liar, and a cheat... So no Rodney, you're nothing like him."[56]

St Pancras New Church is located next to the Euston Road, in London NW1. On the walls of the church are a number of monuments with epitaphs. There is one to William Kitchiner who died in 1827. The monument was erected by his son.

In the wording it says

> *Possessing a heart of unbounded kindness united to an intellect of singular acuteness, diligence and comprehensiveness whose life was an epitome of that beautiful spirit or Christianity which teaches us to be humble, lowly, trusting in God.*

Projects have a start, a middle and an end. During the project, in particular when times are difficult, we will encounter different traits and behaviours from our colleagues.

How will we react in times of trouble? As Epictus said:

> 'Circumstances don't make the man, they only reveal him to himself.'

The project will come to an end and after closing the project we may never see our project team again.

Consider then how will you be remembered? What would your epitaph be if it were written by the people who worked with you? Will you be remembered as a Robbie Robdal type character?

Or instead accorded praise similar to William Kitchiner saying you were:

... of good character, hardworking, caring, diligent, kind and respectful of others, a team player who treated everyone with courtesy and common decency, professional in every way, a person who others were proud to be associated with.

31. The Good Project Samaritan

The Parable of the Good Samaritan

> *The parable of the Good Samaritan is a didactic story told by Jesus in Luke 10:25–37. It is about a traveller (who may or may not have been a Jew) who is stripped of clothing, beaten, and left half dead alongside the road. First a priest and then a Levite comes by, but both avoid the man. Finally, a Samaritan comes by. Samaritans and Jews generally despised each other, but the Samaritan helps the injured man*[57].

Project team formation

Projects have a project team, that core group of people who are responsible for delivery. How was the team put together? A request for volunteers put out, the individuals had some availability, it was expected that this would be delivered in parallel with business as usual. In none of these cases were skills considered.

The project begins. The stronger more vocal team members get involved and actively participate. Time to get work completed is limited. Milestone dates are looming and work has to be done.

The culture

What is the culture of the organisation? Is it dog-eat-dog where people will do anything to be successful, one where to admit failing is career suicide? Now we might see someone failing, not delivering their work when meant to, and struggling to survive, to keep up.

What to do?

Viktor Frankl, author of 'Man's Search for Meaning', identified that individuals have a freedom of choice[58], the ability to choose our response to a situation. He went on to conclude that 'there are only two races of men, decent men and indecent'[59].

So what do we do when a team member is struggling? Do we criticise them, make their life more difficult, seeking to make political gain for their troubles, bad mouthing them to their peers?

Or instead act like the Good Samaritan, offering a helping hand, providing guidance and support, encouragement and education?

Someday?

Someday we may find ourselves or a member of our family in such a situation. Would we want the Good 'Project' Samaritan to be there, to act in a decent way?

32. Planning Definition

Planning[60]

Planning determines what is to be delivered, how much it will cost, when it will be delivered, how it will be delivered and who will carry it out.

33. Heaven can wait, playing to the whistle

'Heaven Can Wait[61] is a 1978 American fantasy-comedy film. It was the second film adaptation of Harry Segall's play of the same name. Warren Beatty plays a quarterback for the American Football team Los Angeles Rams. His character is involved in a car accident whilst out riding a bicycle. He gets taken to heaven, mistakenly, by an over-anxious guardian angel.[62] He returns to earth to take on the body of millionaire industrialist Leo Farnsworth, who has just been murdered by his wife and her lover; much to their surprise coming back to life.

Whilst in the body of Leo Farnsworth he has an argument with the Board of Directors of Leo's company about the importance of future planning. Giving the analogy of American Football, he explains that when play starts 'the quarter back throws the ball downfield to an eligible receiving player'[63]. Now if there is no player down the field, they cannot complete the play and will lose control of the ball.

In project management we can be asked 'why project planning?' In American Football, and also in the UK game of Football, if the ball is passed down the pitch it needs to be received by someone. How will we know if they are there? By pre-planning, agreeing who is going to take which position on the field of play, and whilst the ball is in play their direction of travel.

Project planning involves bringing together the resources. For IT Business solutions this means people, software, hardware, and infrastructure. The project plan identifies where the start date is, and the expected finish date. Like football things may change whilst the project is progressing. Individual behaviours vary, activities may take longer than planned (Late Finish) or complete before the expected date (Early Finish). How do we deal with these changes? In UK Football the term to 'play to the whistle ' means 'to keep playing until you hear the referee blow his whistle to stop the game'[64]. It is not a rule in the game but represents the spirit of the game.

What is the spirit in the project if the work finishes early? To go home and rest? To deliver more than is in the project business case?

Warren Beatty tells us to plan, to be prepared to catch the ball, to be in the correct place ready. In UK Soccer we play to the whistle. Project management involves planning, preparing the resources to move in the right direction, setting the spirit of the project, and then continuing to deliver until advised otherwise.

34. The Richter Scale & seismic impact of a day of work

When planning projects we consider the risks to delivery, the scope of work and who needs to be involved. Projects may be assessed by size. Big projects require big plans, many project management days, lots of thought to go into arranging the resources. This is likely to be the case. Yet what about booking a single day of consultancy? What could be simpler after all it is just a day?

A real life example

We are providing a technical consultant to connect our Spend Management Solution across domains, between different public sector organisations, using the Microsoft Technology Active Directory Federation Services (ADFS). The connectivity is a critical element of the project delivery.

There are four organisations to bring together.

1. Touchstone Spend Management: providing the technical consultant and also an application consultant
2. The system provider: a customer of Touchstone Spend Management who have the software installed
3. The connecting organisation: a new customer of Touchstone Spend Management who will be connecting to the Proactis software at the system provider
4. The ADFS technical specialists: an external organisation providing technical expertise on how to successfully use ADFS to connect Windows Domains.

Let us identify the individuals by role.

1. Touchstone Spend Management: 4 people
    a. Project manager for resource planning
    b. Technical consultant for connectivity between Proactis and ADFS
    c. Application consultant to confirm the Proactis software functions
    d. Account manager: to agree commercial terms

2. The system provider: 7 people
    a. Project manager for resource planning
    b. IT Infrastructure representative to ensure the approach is consistent with the overall connection
    c. IT Network representative to configure the link to an outside domain
    d. IT Security Specialist to agree to the connection from an outside party and sign off that this will not compromise the overall security
    e. Application user to agree that the connection of the new user base will not affect current operations
    f. Vetting department to confirm the relevant consultants have passed the required vetting and security procedures
    g. Project Executive to give authority for the work to proceed and the spend of the money

3. The connecting organisation: 7 people
    a. Project manager for resource planning
    b. IT Infrastructure representative to ensure the approach is consistent with the overall connection from the connecting organisations viewpoint
    c. IT Network representative to confirm the linking to an outside domain
    d. IT Security Specialist to agree to the connection to an outside party will not compromise the overall approach
    e. Vetting department to confirm the relevant consultants have passed the required vetting and security procedures
    f. Application user to test that the connection to the external system work
    g. Project Executive to give authority for the work to proceed and the spend of the money
4. The ADFS technical specialists: 1 person
    a. Technical specialist to provide specific advice on using ADFS and connecting two domains

How can we measure this complexity? By using the Helmsman Scale.

'The Helmsman Scale is designed to mimic the Richter Earthquake scale in terms of significance. Projects are evaluated against criteria in five main areas'[65]:

1. Context Complexity
2. People Complexity
3. Ambiguity
4. Technical Challenge
5. Project Management Challenge

The Scale notes for Technical Challenge

> 'The Technical challenge faced by a project is often given the most attention. ... It is a critical driver of complexity. Helmsman measures technical complexity by looking at the definition, history of development and number of core subsystems expected in the final solution. In addition the previous experience of subsystems integration is evaluated to understand the complexity challenge of the systems integration required.'[66]

The connection may take only a day to deliver. There are 19 people required to be aligned for this single day to be successful, plus operating systems, connectivity software, application software and infrastructure. Typically technical specialists are booked 6 to 8 weeks in advance. Success and the project continues. Problems and the project is delayed 6 to 8 weeks. The project business case identified that each 4 week delay cost the organisation £25,000. An 8 week delay is £50,000.

Now consider as Project Manager reporting back to the Project Board an 8 week delay due to problems with 'a day of work'. The implications are a financial cost £50,000.

On what level of the Richter Scale would be their response? Similar to a Magnitude 5 at 2 terajoules or perhaps a Magnitude 7 at 2 petajoules? Would the room shake as you gave your presentation?

An earthquake may only take one day, its impact a lot longer to recover from. When planning remember Charles Richter. Consider the impact of not planning correctly, and remember to identify who and what is required to successfully complete each day of your project?

35. Project Managers are Anarchists & Punk Rockers

Anarchism	Project Management
Anti-authoritarianism[67]: Anti-authoritarians usually believe in full equality before the law and strong civil liberties. Sometimes the term is used interchangeably with anarchism, an ideology which entails opposing authority or hierarchical organization in the conduct of human relations, including the state system	Project management encourages a diversity of opinion, the right of individuals to make their point during debate, being inclusive of stakeholders views and thoughts. Hierarchical authority is replaced by a matrix structure including the use of meritocracy.
Anti-establishment views[68]: An anti-establishment view or belief is one which stands in opposition to the conventional social, political, and economic principles of a society	Project management questions the established views and beliefs. Project delivery may require fundamental change in an organisation and the political structure.

Anarchism	Project Management
Consensus Democracy[69]*:* Consensus democracy … is characterized by a decision-making structure which involves and takes into account as broad a range of opinions as possible…	Stakeholders are identified, consulted and informed.
Direct action[70]*:* Direct action occurs when a group takes an action which is intended to reveal an existing problem, highlight an alternative, or demonstrate a possible solution to a social issue	Project management involves the setting up of a temporary organisation, the Project, whose role is to take direct action in bringing about change, highlight issues, and demonstrate alternative solutions.
DIY Ethic[71]*:* The abbreviation DIY is also widely used in the military as a way to teach commanders or other types of units to take responsibility, so that they'd be able to do things themselves just as a preparation for their own future.	Projects tend to have finite resources. Project Managers have to be able to make do with what they have available, be resourceful and at times 'roll up their sleeves' to do the work.

Anarchism	Project Management
Freethought[72]*:* Freethought is a philosophical viewpoint that holds opinions should be formed on the basis of logic, reason, and empiricism, rather than authority, tradition, or other dogmas	Projects encourage freethought. The open sharing of ideas. Design work brings together disparate views. Conclusions are based on reasoning out sound argument, observing events and logical analysis
Not selling out[73]*:* In political movements a "sellout" is a person or group claiming to adhere to one ideology, only to follow these claims up with actions contradicting them, such as a revolutionary group claiming to fight for a particular cause, but failing to continue this upon obtaining power.	Project management encourages openness of thinking, to look for an optimal answer, not being dogmatic about staying with a singular approach. The end state will be different from the starting point. To return to the status quo is not an option

Anarchism	Project Management
Question authority[74]... is intended to encourage people to avoid fallacious appeals to authority	Project management involves the questioning of authority, the use of dictatorial approaches is a failing from leaders.
Social Insertion[75]*:* Social insertion consists simply of building a base for anarchist ideas through involvement at rank and file level over time in workplace and community organizations and struggles	Project management actively encourages the participation of a wider community. Project team members are encouraged to go out and promote the benefits of their project, to sell the message that it is the right thing to do.

Punk	Project Management
Punk rock (or "punk") is a rock music genre. Punk bands typically produced short or fast-paced songs, with hard-edged melodies and singing styles, stripped-down instrumentation, and often political, anti-establishment lyrics. Punk embraces a DIY ethic; many bands self-produce recordings and distribute them through informal channel[76]	Projects are activities with a short time period, limited budget, of a political nature, and question authority. They embrace do it yourself, and distribute information through formal and informal channels.
Punk politics cover the entire political spectrum. Punk-related ideologies are mostly concerned with individual freedom and anti-establishment views. Common punk viewpoints include anti-authoritarianism, a DIY ethic, non-conformity, direct action and not selling out.[77]	Project management covers the entire spectrum of organisational politics. They encourage individual freedoms and questioning of the establishment. Activities consist of direct action against the current situation, pursuit of an objective and not selling out.

36. Risk Definition

Risk Management.

The board has ultimate responsibility for risk management and internal control, including for the determination of the nature and extent of the principal risks it is willing to take to achieve its strategic objectives and for ensuring that an appropriate culture has been embedded throughout the organisation[78].

It is the role of management to implement and take day-to-day responsibility for board policies on risk management and internal control. But the board needs to satisfy itself that management has understood the risks, implemented and monitored appropriate policies and controls, and are providing the board with timely information so that it can discharge its own responsibilities. In turn, management should ensure internal responsibilities and accountabilities are clearly established, understood and embedded at all levels of the organisation. Employees should understand their responsibility for behaving according to the culture[79].

37. Risk, Captain Kirk, and Good Governance.

'... I must point out that the possibilities, the potential for knowledge and advancement is equally great. Risk. Risk is our business. That's what this starship is all about'[80].

Captain James Tiberius Kirk, starship USS Enterprise

Captain Kirk, at the end of talking with his team, closes by saying 'they could dissent without prejudice'[81]

So where are the risks?

At project initiation and during delivery we need to assess and regularly review risks. We can identify those that are less likely to occur based on our experience and ask of the project team their views. Yet is the biggest risk a cultural one?

In a BBC News article published in September 2017 about Northern Rock, Gary Hoffman who was brought in as Chief Executive of Northern Rock says:

> *"The management had completely lost touch with the coal face, and did not know what was happening. There was an attitude that you did not question what was going on, which was a tragedy because there were extremely good people at the bank*[82]*."*

The content of the programme or project risk register needs to represent reality, not contain a list of shallow, trite, superficial items that add no substance and are without gravitas. To do this may require the asking of difficult questions, and for those asking the questions to be confident they can do so without fear of retribution or blame from those who now need to listen. They will require the support of the Programme Executive or the Project Executive, who themselves will be working within the culture of the organisation[83].

Conclusion

As project professionals, by understanding the corporate culture, we can assess the project risks in a wider context: working with the Project Board to create an environment in which it is acceptable for individuals to raise their views on potential risks, to be able to comment, as Captain Kirk notes 'without prejudice'. By doing so we are reducing the chance of failure. Risks can be expected, considered, identified, understood, managed and mitigated.

The project team will have a more realistic assessment of the challenges ahead and greater confidence in the plans for successful delivery.

38. If it looks like a duck

If it looks like a duck, and quacks like a duck, we have at least to consider the possibility that we have a small aquatic bird of the family anatidae on our hands[84]

Why risk analysis?

At the start of the project we will perform a risk assessment. For those who are not project professionals the reason for this:

'Risk taking in projects is inevitable since projects are enablers of change and change introduces uncertainty, hence risk. Management of risk should be systematic and not based on chance. It is about the proactive identification, assessment and control of risks that might affect the delivery of the project's objectives'[85]

Types of projects

Projects fall into different types. Classifications such as Runners, Repeaters and Strangers, or Quest, Movie, Painting by Numbers, Fog[86] and so forth. With the delivery of business solutions there are projects that are performed regularly. Examples of these are upgrades from one version to another, system redesign, implementation of a new module within an existing suite.

So a new project comes along and what do we do? We look for similarities on work that has been performed previously. However 'Once people have started thinking about a problem one way, the same mental circuits or pathways get activated and strengthened each time they think about it. This facilitates the retrieval of information. These same pathways, however, also become the mental ruts that make it difficult to reorganize the information mentally so as to see it from a different perspective[87]'

For example consider this project

It is an upgrade of a finance system from one version to another, with no changes to the chart of accounts. The latest version that has been available for a period of time (so this will not be an early adopter project), the changes to the screen layouts and structure are minimal. The reason for the project is that the legacy version is going out of mainstream support.

When we perform our risks assessment prior experience tells us that a number of risks can be mitigated or are not risks at all.

For example:

- There are a number of specialist consultants who understand the software functionality. Skills are not based on a limited pool or single person dependency.
- It is installed at many other locations. Therefore it is proven in other live environments.
- It uses what can be considered standard infrastructure (Microsoft Windows Server, Microsoft SQL Server, IIS) and skills in these areas are widely available.
- There are no changes to the chart of account structure. This significantly simplifies the data migration which will use in built functionality to migrate from one version to another.
- The users are experienced in the existing software so will only need training in new features.
- The method of integration has not changed so any interfaces will need repointing not re-writing.

Sounds easy, like painting by numbers. Now a duck has two legs, feathers, quacks, floats on water, and can fly. We see it looks like a duck and behaves like a duck[88].

Projects might look similar. They may have characteristics seen before. Yet they are not ducks. There are nuances to consider, people issues to understand, timelines, holidays to be taken, environment issues, other projects taking precedence, legal considerations, business as usual that is likely to take priority, and so the list goes on.

Conclusion

When we do our risk assessment, it takes mental strength not to fall into the trap of thinking this was easy before, and it will be easy now. Certainly we can draw comfort that the project has some similarities. From this to then probe into what is different, what are the esoteric points to consider?

39. Miscellaneous

The following section contains a selection of blogs which cover various categories

40. The laws of the game

The rules of football are officially referred to as the "Laws of the Game"[89]. There are 17 laws in total and are described very precisely on the FIFA web site[90].

Could these be mapped to project delivery?

Laws of the game	Project
01 Field of play	The environment in which the project is delivered.
02 The Ball	The ultimate project objective which is kicked around during project delivery
03 The Players	The project team
04 The Players' Equipment	Project plans, communication technologies
05 The Referee	The project executive
06 The Other Match Officials	The project manager, the senior users
07 The Duration of the Match	Agreed at project initiation
08 The Start and Restart of Play	Play starts when initiation is completed. Restart of play is after a Project Exception or End Stage meeting

Laws of the game	Project
09 The Ball In and Out of Play	The project stops when it is out of tolerance
10 Determining the Outcome of a Match	Has the business case been delivered?
11 Off side	When a team member tries to promote their own objective without due consideration of others
12 Fouls and Misconduct	Team behaviours that are deemed unacceptable such as confrontation, bullying, abusive language
13 Free Kicks	Services provided by a supplier to make good on wasted effort.
14 The Penalty Kick	Supplier or customer gets an opportunity for significant advantage over the other if played correctly.
15 The Throw-In	Restarting the project after an exception report has been raised.
16 The Goal Kick	Moving the project forward quickly through gaining an early project success
17 The Corner Kick	A chance to gain advantage over the naysayers and cynics.

41. User stories and Business Intelligence

What are user stories?

A user story is a tool used … to capture a description of a software feature from an end-user perspective. The user story describes the type of user, what they want and why. A user story helps to create a simplified description of a requirement[91].

Why user stories?

In Business Intelligence implementations there are a multitude of options for the preparation of reports. The BIRST software solution, for example, provides six ways for delivery of this information.

Yet where to start? If this is a new implementation of a BI reporting solution, the user is unaware of the options available. Asking a question such as 'What do you want to see' they are likely to answer 'Well what can it do?' which will result in a circular discussion.

Instead by following the user story option, the individual says what their need is. As the specialist provider of Business Intelligence we interpret this and build an appropriate solution for walk through.

An example

The Services Director says

I want to .....

see the services revenue forecast and margin forecast by month for the coming six months with a drill down by business unit . The information content including cost centre, employee name, client name, expected revenue, expected margin, month and year of booking. The report to work like a pivot table in MS Excel where I can move the data around to give a multi-dimensional analysis

So that

I can see if we are going to meet our revenue targets and margin targets or whether sales effort is needed.

What this means?

A list of user stories is prepared. These are prioritised and a budget allocated against each report. One by one the reports are developed, presented to the user for feedback and then refined. Upfront we agree a fixed number of reviews and a time-line for the overall development. At the end of each of the reviews, the report is handed over to use in a live environment. In this way the elapsed delivery time is reduced. We do not wait until all the reports are written. You get the business value quickly.

So consider for yourselves, what are the critical reports you need now? Write down a user story for each starting with

> I want to …
>
> So that …

TouchstoneBI will interpret this into how best to deliver the information to you.

42. Art is never finished, only abandoned

Leonardo DaVinci is attributed with saying these words about art. He was likely to be thinking that every painting could always be improved. The colours not quite right, the expression on faces needing a few changes, the perspective improved, a model requiring subtle adjustments and refinements.

What are we trying to achieve with the project? The outcomes will be defined in the business case. They may be financial such as increasing revenue, non-financial including risk reduction, process improvements, and better management information. The project will have a budget and a time-line for delivery.

Consider a business intelligence implementation. The provision of analytics might be the first time that such information is put on the desktop of directors and managers. They have identified the requirement through the preparation of user stories. These are interpreted by the delivery team and a potential solution presented in a structured review. Feedback is given and a further iteration of development and review takes place. Yet how many reviews and changes should there be?

Traditional project management uses the triangle of time, cost and quality. How much time is there, with what money to produce the correct deliverables of the requisite quality? Yet what if the deliverable cannot be defined upfront? There still needs to be limits on the project otherwise it will never end.

For a new implementation we need to change our frame of reference. Let us fix the time and fix the budget. There is a finite amount of time during which there will be development of our business intelligence reports. Each one will be written, reviewed, updated and further reviewed. This will continue through a list, based on a prioritisation or requirements, until the time constraint ends, or the budget is spent.

The advantage is that it focuses the individual. They are not given the luxury of continual changes of mind. There is an end date after which development ceases and the functionality is passed into the production environment. The users get to use the reports.

The artist needs to stop painting. Da Vinci suggested it was abandoned. In project delivery the work is not abandoned, it is taken to an agreed point.

Parkinson's law states that work expands to fill the time available. Let us limit the time, prioritise the requirements, develop a work breakdown structure to agree the full scope of the project and deliver a (project) work of art.

43. 3 Michelin Stars Projects

What if projects were assessed like a menu in a restaurant? How would it be worded?

Our offering

We believe in recruiting specially chosen project team members, with hand crafted software written by world class companies. Work can be undertaken on a single site, across multiple sites, different time zones through the world delivered a la carte or to a set menu.

Starters

Why not commence your journey with a simple business process review, or a technical assessment of the infrastructure? This is a unique one-to-one service.

Alternatively you may prefer to start with a single module implementation to enhance your existing system: an efficient bank reconciliation module, an elegant advanced inquiry solution, or an asset module to value your capital investments.

Sharers

Organisations do not work in isolation, and you may be considering the end to end issues. Our sharer service will work with you and one or more of your business partners to identify integration process improvements.

Solutions delivery

The pièce de résistance of our services comes with full solutions delivery. Bringing together the finest software ingredients, sourced from world class authors, seasoned with experience project personnel, delivered to your door with style and finesse, enabling the full return of your investment.

This can be tailored from one application (such as finance or procurement), or for the more adventurous multiple modules implemented across different parts of the organisation. Software solutions include finance, procurement, spend control, customer relationship management, business analytics, planning, forecasting, and document management to name but a few.

Choosing from such a wide selection can be difficult, so to help you select we have put together some suggestions:

- The Directors choice: business intelligence, planning, business analytics,
- The Finance choice: finance system, Financial and management reporting, budgeting, forecasting,
- The Procurement choice: purchase to pay, eRequisitions, auctions, contract management, supplier relationship management
- The Users choice: process improvement, job enrichment, motivational benefits, customer relationship management

Desserts

Finish your project with a three month or six month benefit investment review.

44. Business Case Definition

The Business Case [92]

The business case provides justification for undertaking a project or programme. It evaluates the benefit, cost and risk of alternative options and provides a rationale for the preferred solution.

45. Monet, Impressionism & project investment appraisal

> "Works of art have many meanings and some have more meanings, but even if all their meanings may never be known to any one observer, his obligation is still to encounter each work from as many aspects of his own intellectual and emotional experience as he can. Because each work of art originates in the mind and feelings of a human being, it reaches its destination in the mind and feelings of another."
>
> George Heard Hamilton[93]

How to evaluate a painting?

To evaluate a painting is more than deciding whether you like it or not. The web site Art Encyclopaedia[94] offers some suggestions on how to appreciate art. These include:

- When was the painting created?
- Is the painting abstract or representational?
- What school of movement is the painting associated with?
- At what point was the artist in his career?
- What was his background?
- What materials were used in the creation of the painting?
- How does the painting compare with others?

Investment Appraisal

The APM Body of Knowledge defines Investment Appraisal[95] as

> *Investment appraisal is a collection of techniques used to identify the attractiveness of an investment.*

It goes on to note there are many factors and does give some guidance. Six areas are listed being financial, legal, environmental, social, operational and risk.

The Business Case will have been prepared by one or more individuals who are likely to have invested much time and effort in researching, considering, interviewing, documenting and drawing together the necessary information before the final version is published. When reviewing the business case, or performing an investment appraisal, what if we were to consider the Business Case as though it were a work of written art that originated in the mind of a human being(s).

The concepts and proposal presented may appear to be abstract to our thinking, perhaps may be contrary to our own or organisations' accepted norms and it may even challenge the way we would ordinarily challenge and our initial reaction therefore is likely to be one of opposition.

Art Historians will advise that the Impressionists 'faced harsh opposition from the conventional art community in France'[96]. Monet was an impressionist. However one of his Water Lilies paintings, on 6 May 2014, 'was auctioned at Christie's, New York City for $27 million'[97] and this after his paintings were sneered at by the critics as reflecting his 'blurred vision'.

When performing an investment appraisal could you be opposing a yet to be highly valued, yet unappreciated, work of art? What if you are using preconceived notions and criteria, perhaps subconsciously, which results in missing the bigger picture? Is it your vision that is blurred?

George Hamilton advises us 'to encounter each work from as many aspects of his own intellectual and emotional experience as he can'. Let us consider the same when we evaluate an investment appraisal.

46. Acres of Diamonds & Business Intelligence

Russell Herman Conwell was an American Baptist Minister, Orator, Philanthropist, Lawyer and Writer[98]. He gave a lecture titled ' Acres of Diamonds ' which is based on a story he heard whilst travelling in the Middle East.

The story is of a farmer in Africa who had heard there were great riches to be made from Diamond Mining. Diamonds are very valuable, and the farmer dreamt of a being wealthy. He could lavish on himself and his family anything they wanted. All he needed to do was find some diamonds and his fortune is made. So the farmer sold his farm. For the next few years he travelled across Africa looking for diamonds. Yet he had no success. He was penniless, destitute and jumped into a river to drown.

Meanwhile the man who bought his farm was walking past a stream and saw a large shiny stone in the water. He picked it up and took it home. The stone was placed on the mantelpiece. One day a visitor to the farmer looked at this stone and explained it was a large diamond. He asked the farmer from whence it came, to which the reply was from a stream on his property. There are many other shiny stones in the water explained the farmer. This was the largest one he saw. The farm was on top of a large diamond deposit.

The moral of the story is that there are likely to be diamonds under your feet. We just need to look for them.

Today's IT systems have been in place for many years. There are large data stores in place. SQL databases with millions of transaction lines waiting to be analysed. Multiple repositories across disparate domains and systems. Each one holding its own riches in information terms. What if we could mine this data? To extract out of it the nuggets and gems of understanding about our business; the unknown unknowns such as who our customers really are as opposed to who we think they are. The SQL databases could be the acres of diamonds in our own business.

TouchstoneBI has the tools to extract this information quickly and efficiently. This can be modelled graphically to provide visual representations, what-if analysis, shown against key performance indicators, delivered to the desktop or mobile, assisting in effective decision making that was not previously possible.

So if you are looking for your acres of diamonds, they are likely to be in your data stores. The riches are in the information waiting to be unearthed. TouchstoneBI has the tools to dig these out and refine them into valuable assets.

47. References

1. Introduction

1. The Full Monty, Dir. Peter Catteneo, 20th Century Fox, Film, 1997

2. Acknowledgements

3. Communication

2. The APM Body of Knowledge, 6th Edition, Association for Project Management, 2012, Print

3. Individual Competence Baseline for Project, Programme and Portfolio Management, Version 4. International Project Management Association

4. A 'Lipsmackin' Communication Strategy

4. A 1970's advert for Pepsi Cola, Advertising Agency: Dave Trott, BMP

5. Article19: Freedom of Expression

5. https://en.wikipedia.org/wiki/Universal_Declaration_of_Human_Rights

6. http://www.un.org/en/universal-declaration-human-rights/

7. https://en.wikipedia.org/wiki/Chatham_House_Rule

6. Henry V and Shakespeare's English

8. http://lingojam.com/shakespearean

9. William Shakespeare, Henry V, Act 4, Scene 3, The English Camp

7. The word 'meeting'

10. https://www.google.co.uk/search?q=definition+of+meeting&oq=definition+of+meeting&aqs=chrome..69i57j0l5.2728j0j4&sourceid=chrome&ie=UTF-8

8. Project communication and Transport for London

9. Communicate, Motivate, Collaborate

11. The Federal Aviation Administration 'Fly the Aircraft First': https://www.faa.gov/news/safety_briefing/2016/media/SE_Topic_16-08.pdf

12. Forsyth, Mark, 2013. The Elements of Eloquence: How to Turn the Perfect English Phrase. Icon Books. Kindle Edition.

13. Kotter, John P, Leading Change, Harvard Business Press, 2012, Print

10. Competence & Knowledge Definitions

14. Individual Competence Baseline for Project, Programme and Portfolio Management, Version 4. International Project Management Association

15. REAL Knowledge at NASA A Knowledge Services Model for the Modern Project Environment Dr. Ed Hoffman Dr. Jon Boyle.

11. Marriages may come and go

16. The Odd Couple, Dir. Gene Saks, Paramount Pictures, Film, 1968

17. A black swan is an event or occurrence that deviates beyond what is normally expected of a situation and is extremely difficult to predict: http://www.investopedia.com/terms/b/blackswan.asp

12. Training: the wider context for delivering improvement

13. Governance & Culture Definitions

18. The APM Body of Knowledge, 6th Edition, Association for Project Management, 2012, Print

19. Corporate Culture and the Role of Boards, Report of Observations, Financial Reporting Council, July 2016

14. Project Culture and the 'Tone from the Top'

20. Corporate Culture and the Role of Boards, Report of Observations, The Financial Reporting Council, 2016

21: FRC, 2016. UK Corporate Governance Code https://www.frc.org.uk/Our-Work/Publications/Corporate-Governance/UKCorporate-Governance-Code-April-2016.pdf

22. The Financial Reporting Council report does note an area for vigilance is in Hierarchical Attitudes.

23. CIPD, 2016. A duty to care? Evidence of the importance of organisational culture to effective governance and leadership

15. The Scapegoat

24. https://en.wikipedia.org/wiki/The_Scapegoat_(painting)

25. For a discussion on Responsible see Covey, Stephen R, The Seven Habits of Highly Effective People , Stephen R Covey, Simon & Schuster UK, 2004, Print

26. 'Derived from the word "Excuse".It is tendency/Disease/Regular behaviour of making excuse for every poor performance. In simpler words, giving excuses for everything and trying to back their faults. 'http://www.urbandictionary.com/tags.php?tag=excusitus

16. Motivation Definition

27. Individual Competence Baseline for Project, Programme and Portfolio Management, Version 4. International Project Management Association

17. A tale of two cities, a tale of two projects

28. https://en.wikiquote.org/wiki/A_Tale_of_Two_Cities

18. The Blues Brothers

29. The Blues Brothers, Dir. John Landis, Universal Pictures, Film, 1980,

30. Individual Competence Baseline for Project, Programme and Portfolio Management, Version 4. International Project Management Association

19. Why be a project professional?

31. https://en.wikipedia.org/wiki/George_Mallory

32. https://www.goodreads.com/author/quotes/3348511.George_Mallory

20. It takes courage to stand alone

33. Rand, Ayn, The Fountainhead, Penguin Classics, 2007, Print

34. Managing Successful Projects with PRINCE2, The Stationery Office; 2009 edition, Print

21. Master of Photography and Banal

35. http://masterofphotography.tv/

22. Newton's Laws of Motion and project momentum

36. https://www.reference.com/science/newton-s-three-laws-motion-103f06122f5ca0cc

37. https://en.wikipedia.org/wiki/Newton's_laws_of_motion#Newton.27s_first_law

38. http://www.kotterinternational.com/the-8-step-process-for-leading-change

23. James Brown & seeing the light with QUBE

39. The Blues Brothers, Dir. John Landis, Universal Pictures, Film, 1980,

40. http://www.pentaclethevbs.com/

41. http://www.pentaclethevbs.com/qube/

24. Interpersonal Skills Definition

42. The APM Body of Knowledge, 6th Edition, Association for Project Management, 2012, Print

25. Guilty of Crimes against Creativity

43. Goleman, Daniel, Working with Emotional Intelligence: Bloomsbury, 1998, Print

44. Ibid. For a discussion on this see pages 103 and 104

26. Fight Director or Peacemaker

45. http://work.chron.com/job-description-fighting-director-26326.html

46. Individual Competence Baseline for Project, Programme and Portfolio Management, Version 4. International Project Management Association

27. The People versus Precision

47. For an explanation on reading a compass see http://www.ubergizmo.com/how-to/read-gps-coordinates/

48. See 'How Hard Can It Be? Actively Managing Complexity in Technology Projects The complexity assessment tool offers a framework for articulating, assessing, and managing sources of complexity in technology projects. Harvey R. Maylor , Neil W. Turner, and Ruth Murray-Webster'

49. From Susan Madsen, https://www.linkedin.com/pulse/socio-political-complexity-project-management-susanne-madsen

50. The Royal Institute of Chartered Surveyors Guidance Note, Stakeholder Engagement 1st Edition, ISBN 978-78321-075-6

51. Mayfield, Patrick, Practical People Engagement, Leading change through the Power of Relationships, 2013, Print

28. There is a lot of washing-up in the sink

52. http://www.ericberne.com/transactional-analysis/

29. Integrity and Reliability Definition

53. Corporate Culture and the Role of Boards, Report of Observations, Financial Reporting Council, July 2016

54. ibid

55. Individual Competence Baseline for Project, Programme and Portfolio Management, Version 4. International Project Management Association

30. Project Manager – Sleepless in Peckham

56. https://en.wikipedia.org/wiki/Sleepless_in_Peckham

31. The Good Project Samaritan

57. https://en.wikipedia.org/wiki/Parable_of_the_Good_Samaritan

58. https://en.wikipedia.org/wiki/Man%27s_Search_for_Meaning

59. ibid

32. Planning Definition

60. The APM Body of Knowledge, 6th Edition, Association for Project Management, 2012, Print

33. Heaven can wait, playing to the whistle

61. Heaven Can Wait, Dir. Warren Beatty, Buck Henry, Paramount Pictures, Film, 1978

62. https://en.wikipedia.org/wiki/Heaven_Can_Wait_(1978_film)

63. https://en.wikipedia.org/wiki/Quarterback

64. http://languagecaster.com/weekly-football-phrase-to-play-to-the-whistle/

34. The Richter Scale & seismic impact of a day of work

65. https://iccpm.com/sites/default/files/kcfinder/files/Guide_to_the_Complexity_Scale_v_1.2.pdf

66. Ibid

35. Project Managers are Anarchists & Punk Rockers

67. https://en.wikipedia.org/wiki/Anti-authoritarianism

68. https://en.wikipedia.org/wiki/Anti-establishment

69.
https://en.wikipedia.org/wiki/Consensus_democracy

70. https://en.wikipedia.org/wiki/Direct_action

71. https://en.wikipedia.org/wiki/Do_it_yourself

72. https://en.wikipedia.org/wiki/Freethought

73. https://en.wikipedia.org/wiki/Selling_out

74.
https://en.wikipedia.org/wiki/Question_authority

75.
https://en.wikipedia.org/wiki/Social_insertion

76. https://en.wikipedia.org/wiki/Punk_rock

77.
https://en.wikipedia.org/wiki/Punk_subculture

36. Risk

78. Guidance on Risk Management, Internal Control and Related Financial and Business Reporting, September 2014. Financial Reporting Council

79. ibid

37. Risk, Captain Kirk, and Good Governance

80. Star Trek, TV Series, Return to Tomorrow (1968) http://www.imdb.com/title/tt0708445/quotes.
81. ibid

82. http://www.bbc.co.uk/news/business-41229513

83. For details on risks, culture and more information see Corporate Culture and the Role of Boards, Report of Observations, The Financial Reporting Council, 2016, page 26

38. If it looks like a duck

84. Adams, Douglas, Dirk Gently's Holistic Detective Agency, Pan, 2012 Print

85. Managing Successful Projects with PRINCE2, The Stationery Office; 2009 edition, Print

86.
http://www.pentacle.co.uk/perfectprojects.htm

87. The Psychology of Intelligence Analysis, Richard J. Heuer, Jr. CIA Publication

88. The RSPB web site (https://www.rspb.org.uk/birds-and-wildlife/bird-and-wildlife-guides/browse-bird-families/swans.aspx) lists different types of duck

39. Miscellaneous

40. The laws of the game

89. http://www.fifa.com/mm/Document/FootballDevelopment/Refereeing/02/79/92/44/Laws.of.the.Game.2016.2017_Neutral.pdf

90. http://rulesoffootball.co.uk/

41. User stories and Business Intelligence

91. http://searchsoftwarequality.techtarget.com/definition/user-story

42. Art is never finished, only abandoned

43. 3 Michelin Stars Projects

44. Business Case

92. The APM Body of Knowledge, 6th Edition, Association for Project Management, 2012, Print

45. Monet, Impressionism & project investment appraisal

93. Hamilton, George Heard, Painting and Sculpture in Europe 1880-1940, Penguin Books, 1989, Print
94. http://www.visual-arts-cork.com/art-evaluation.htm
95. APM Body of Knowledge, 6th Edition.
96. https://en.wikipedia.org/wiki/Impressionism
97. https://en.wikipedia.org/wiki/Water_Lilies_(Monet_series)#The_paintings_at_auction

46. Acres of Diamonds & Business Intelligence

98. https://en.wikipedia.org/wiki/Russell_Conwell

48. Index

'Aviate, Navigate, Communicate, 30
A Tale of Two Cities, 46
Acres of Diamonds, 118, 134
ADFS, 86, 87, 88
Adult, 74, 75, 76
Africa, 118
Ambiguity, 89
American Football, 84
Anarchists, 91, 130
anatidae, 99
and Sydney Carton, 46
Anti-authoritarianism, 91
Anti-establishment, 91
APM, 13, 116, 120, 123, 127, 130, 133, 134
Arsenal, 15
Art of War, 22
Article 19, 21
Association for Project Management, 13
Ayn Rand, 52
Banal, 55, 56, 126
BBC, 79, 97
Beer, 12
BIRST, 106
Blues Brothers, 48, 61, 125
Body of Knowledge, 116, 120, 123, 127, 130, 133
Business Case, 114, 116, 133
Business Intelligence, 106, 118, 133, 134
Captain James Tiberius Kirk, 97
Catholic, 48
Charles Darnay, 46
Charles Dickens, 46
Chatham House, 22
Child, 74, 75, 76
Christie's, 116
Communication, 18, 19, 20, 76, 120
Consensus Democracy, 92
Context Complexity, 89
Creative, 56, 63
Culture, 38, 39, 40, 41, 123, 124, 129, 132
Dailymotion, 19
Dalai Lama, 63
Dan Aykroyd, 48
Diamond, 118
Direct action, 92
duck, 99, 101, 132
Eddie Obeng, 60
Emotional Intelligence, 127

Epictus, 34, 80
Eric Berne, 74
Ethical, 77
Euston Road, 79
Evaluation, 63, 64
Everest, 50
excusitus, 43
Facebook, 19
Facetime, 19
Felix Unger, 33
FIFA, 104
Fight Director, 67, 127
Financial Reporting Council, 39, 77, 123, 124, 129, 132
First Law of Motion, 57
Freethought, 93, 131
Gary Hoffman, 97
General Assembly, 21
George Heard Hamilton, 115
George Herbert Leigh Mallory, 50
Gmail, 19
Good Samaritan, 81, 82
Google[1], 25
Governance, 38, 39, 40, 97, 123, 124, 132
Gower Handbook of Programme Management, 13
Gregorian, 70
Harvard Business School, 63
Hayes Manual, 71
Heaven Can Wait[1], 84
Helmsman Scale, 88, 89
Henry V, 23, 121
Hijri, 70
IIS, 101
Impressionism, 115, 134
Individual Competence Baseline, 48, 68, 120, 122, 125, 127, 129
Informix 4GL, 12
Instagram, 19
Institute of Sales Management, 13
Integrity, 77, 78, 129
International Project Management Association, 48, 122, 125, 129
Interpersonal Skills, 62, 127
Investment Appraisal, 116
Jake Blues, 61
James Brown, 48, 49, 60, 61, 127
John Belushi, 48
John Kotter, 30, 58, 59
John Landis, 48
Kafka, 12
Knowledge, 32, 122, 134
Laws of the Game, 104
Leo Farnsworth, 84
Leonardo DaVinci, 109
Leviticus', 42
LinkedIn, 19
Lipsmackin', 19, 20, 120
London, 27, 69, 79
Los Angeles Rams, 84

Man's Search for Meaning', 82
Managing Successful Programmes, 13
Master of Photography, 55, 126
Member of the Association for Project Management, 13
Member of the Institute of Directors, 13
Michelin, 111, 133
Microsoft, 23, 25, 70, 86, 101
Microsoft Word, 25
mobile phone, 19, 29, 69
Monet, 115, 116, 134
Motivation, 32, 45, 125
National Grid, 77
New York City, 116
Newton, 57, 58, 59, 126
Northern Rock, 97
Oliviero Toscani, 55
OneNote, 19
Only Fools and Horses, 79
Overcontrol, 64, 65
Palais de Chaillot, 21
Parable, 81, 129
Parent, 74, 75, 76
Paris, 21
Parkinson's law, 110
Peacemaker, 67, 127
Peckham, 79, 129
People Complexity, 89
petajoules, 90
photography, 13
Planning, 83, 130
play to the whistle, 85
poker, 33, 34
PRINCE2, 53, 126, 132
Proactis, 23, 24, 86, 87
Project Board, 40, 53, 54, 90, 98
Project Executive, 53, 87, 88, 98
Pulp Fiction, 12
Punk, 91, 95, 130
Punk rock, 95
Punk Rockers, 91, 130
QUBE, 60, 61, 127
Relentless deadlines, 64
Relentless Deadlines, 65
Richter, 86, 89, 90, 130
RICS, 72
risk, 30, 53, 63, 64, 65, 77, 96, 97, 98, 99, 102, 109, 114, 116
Robbie Robdal, 79, 80
Rodney Trotter, 79
Russell Herman Conwell, 118
Scapegoat, 42, 124
Second Law of Motion, 58
Senior Supplier, 53
Senior Users, 53
Shakespeare, 23, 24, 121
Shakespeare's, 23, 24, 121
SharePoint, 19

Sir Peter Gershon, 77
Sir Winfried Bischoff, 77
Sky TV, 55
Skype, 19
Snapchat, 19
Social Insertion, 94
Socio Political', 71
Spend Control, 53, 86, 87
SQL Server, 101
St Pancras New Church, 79
Sun Tzu, 22
Supplier Engagement, 35
Supplier Relationship Management, 35
Surveillance, 63, 64
Technical Challenge, 89
Teresa Amabile, 63
TFL, 27
Thai Buddhist, 70
The Fountainhead, 52
The Odd Couple, 33
the Second World War, 21
TouchstoneBI, 108, 119
TouchstoneCRM, 16
TouchstoneEnergy, 16
TouchstoneFMS, 12, 16, 53, 69
TouchstoneProactis, 16
Transport for London, 27, 28, 122
Triple Rock Baptist Church, 48
Tumblr, 19
UDHR, 21
United Nations, 21
Universal Declaration of Human Rights, 21
UNIX, 12
USS Enterprise, 97
Viktor Frankl, 82
Vimeo, 19
Warren Beatty, 84, 85
Water Lilies, 116
WebEx, 19
WhatsApp, 19
William Kitchiner, 79, 80
Xing, 19
Yahoo, 19
Yammer, 19
YouTube, 19, 36